India and the Hellenistic World

Hindu Tradition Series

The Hindu Tradition Series aims to bring together books of the highest academic standard that critically interrogate Hindu tradition in the widest sense. Its focus is on cultural and religious history, including relevant political and social developments. The interaction with other traditions, whether originally from inside or outside the Indian subcontinent, will figure prominently among its volumes.

4

Foreword by the General Editor

The cultural interaction between India and the Hellenistic world does not usually receive the attention it deserves. Scholars go on trying to derive features of classical Hinduism from the Veda, without seriously taking into consideration that parts of the subcontinent were once ruled by Greeks, whose culture exerted a profound influence in its new environment.

It is therefore a matter of joy that a reprint of the book *India and the Hellenistic World* is now coming out in the Hindu Tradition Series. This book provides readers with an authoritative presentation of the relevant historical data, and thus allows them to familiarize themselves with an important but much neglected aspect of the Hindu tradition.

India and the Hellenistic World

by

Klaus Karttunen

MOTILAL BANARSIDASS PUBLISHERS
PRIVATE LIMITED • DELHI

First Indian Edition : Delhi, ***2017***

Published in arrangement with
FINNISH ORIENTAL SOCIETY
Suomen Itämainen Seura
Finska Orientsällskapet
C/o Department of World Cultures
P.O. Box 59 (Unioninkatu 38 B)
00014 Helsingin Yliopisto

ISBN: 978-81-208-4100-0

Available at
MOTILAL BANARSIDASS
41 U.A., Bungalow Road, Jawahar Nagar, Delhi 110 007
8 Mahalaxmi Chamber, 22 Bhulabhai Desai Road, Mumbai 400 026
203 Royapettah High Road, Mylapore, Chennai 600 004
236, 9th Main III Block, Jayanagar, Bangalore 560 011
8 Camac Street, Kolkata 700 017
Ashok Rajpath, Patna 800 004
Chowk, Varanasi 221 001

MLBD Cataloging-in-Publication Data
India and the Hellenistic World by Klaus Karttunen
Includes References and General Index
ISBN: 978-81-208-4100-0
I. History II. Indian and Greek Literature.
III. Hellenistic World. IV. Karttunen, Klaus

Published by
Motilal Banarsidass Publishers Private Limited
www.mlbd.com • mlbd@mlbd.com
Printed by Nice Printing Press

PREFACE

In 1989, when I published my doctoral dissertation, entitled *India in Early Greek Literature*, I had no clear idea as to how exactly I would go on with my Graeco-Indian studies. Soon enough, however, I decided to go on where I had stopped, chronologically, and discuss Graeco-Indian relations throughout their history. In this plan, *India in Early Greek Literature* is the first volume, and now I present volume Two, *India and the Hellenistic World*. In the first volume I have discussed the Greek accounts of India and the relations between India and Greece until Alexander's Indian campaign. Later authors, like Megasthenes, were mentioned only when their information was relevant for this purpose. This time my focus is on the Hellenistic period in the narrow sense of the word, from Alexander to the rise of Roman Imperial hegemony. I am presently working on volume Three, *India and the Roman West,* which I hope to be able to conclude within a few years. If all goes well a fourth volume on late Antiquity will conclude the series. A side issue of this is a separate volume dealing with the Yonas and Yavanas (both originally signifying Greeks) in Indian literature.

The main object of my plan is to collect, explain and discuss the relevant passages in Greek and Latin literature in their relation to Greek and Roman society and literary traditions as well as to the then existing information about India and other Asian countries, in some cases Africa too. My methods are philological, but I have also made an earnest attempt to find out and utilize the new evidence offered by such disciplines as archaeology, epigraphy, and numismatics. The importance of the new finds in Central Asia/Afghanistan/Pakistan, in South India/Sri Lanka, and to a lesser degree in Egypt is so great that it cannot be ignored even in a philological study. I can only beg the pardon of specialists in these fields – many of whom have actually been very helpful – if I have blundered somewhere because of my ignorance of some finer points of methodology.

Often I have had to give in to the sheer impossibility of keeping strict chronological boundaries. We are not always able to decide what belongs to the Hellenistic (in the narrow sense) or the Roman period, or both, and there is some necessary overlapping between the present volume and the future book about Rome. This can be seen especially in chapters IV and V, where all information culled from the literature of the Roman period has been included and only late authors like Cosmas are deemed too late. Reviewers are welcome to reproach me, but this seemed to be the only reasonable course of action. After all, much of what has been said e.g. by Pliny and Aelianus without any reference to the source, clearly hails from the Hellenistic period, but here too it is impossible to draw a clear boundary.

Of course, I could have modified my title in order to make it correspond more closely to all the chapters of the book, but then I would probably have ended up with something very complicated. And though some critics seem to appreciate it, I do not like to return to the colophon-like titles of many lines in length that were used in the 16th century (when they actually represented the first phase in an evolution from mediaeval colophon to modern title). And even allowing myself these slips from strict chronology, I shall have enough interesting questions to discuss in the next book, *India and the Roman West.* To balance the two volumes I have also left the vexed question of possible influences or interaction in the sphere of philosophy and religion to the next volume. Those colleagues who would like to know my opinion as to whether Scepticism was influenced by Indian philosophy, or Pāśupata by Greek philosophy, will thus have to wait.

A large part of this work was written in Freiburg in Germany, where I had the opportunity to spend two periods, in 1991/92 and 1994/95 as an Alexander von Humboldt scholarship holder. My deepest thanks go therefore to the Alexander von Humboldt Foundation. They not only financed my stay in Germany, but were ready to help in many kinds of material problems connected with my work. The rest of the work has been financed by the Finnish Academy. From January 1994 I have been a full-time Research Fellow of the Academy and in this position I am also able to continue with the next volume.

Next my thanks are due to my generous host in Freiburg, Professor O. von Hinüber, who has, in addition to the free use of his Department and personal library, read a large part of a preliminary version of the manuscript and offered very valuable comments. Especially I have benefited from his profound knowledge of MIA.

Some parts of this book and related matters I have been able to discuss in guest lectures (in Cracow, Gothenburg, Groningen, Halle, Lyons, Naples, Rome, St. Petersburg, Stockholm), in sessions of the South Asian Archaeology Conferences (in Berlin, Helsinki and Cambridge) and in the Finnish Society of Classical Philology, and I have often received valuable comments.

A great number of colleagues have sent me their publications or given their advice. Especially I should like to mention here U. P. Arora (Bareilly), O. Bopearachchi (Paris), P. Callieri (Rome and Bologna), M. R. Cimino (Rome), P. Daffinà (Rome), A. Dihle (Heidelberg), H. Falk (Berlin), E. Garzilli (Perugia), T. Marszewski (Cracow), H. P. Ray (Delhi), J. Sachse (Wrocław), J.-F. Salles (Lyons), R. Salomon (Seattle), F. F. Schwarz (Graz), M. Taddei (Rome and Naples), and D. P. E. Weerakkody (Peradeniya). My thanks can no longer reach P. H. L. Eggermont (1914–1995).

Without the help of J. Vasil'kov (St.Petersburg) and A. Vigasin (Moscow) several important Russian contributions would have been missing from my sources. Special mention must also be made of J.-F. Salles for offering a preprint of De Romanis' book, and of Stefan Faller (Freiburg), who helped greatly with sources concerning Sri Lanka. It was with hesitation that I wrote my chapter about Sri Lanka as I know that both Mr. Faller's dissertation and Dr. Weerakkody's monograph on the subject will be appearing shortly.

I must also thank my friends Bertil Tikkanen and Martti Leiwo for talking and listening. I have often obtained wider perspectives in the meetings of the Finnish Society of the History of Learning. Mr. Pertti Seppälä has kindly helped me to quote uniformly in the

Pinyin system the few Chinese names mentioned, and my brother, Krister Karttunen, has checked numerous botanical names for chapter V.1.

Michael Cox, Lic. Theol., has kindly checked and patiently corrected my English and in addition offered his advice about the few Hebrew words discussed by me.

Finally I must express my deepest thanks to my wife Tuula, and my two sons, Einar and Reino. While for me the work often involved so much fun and enjoyment, they could only see the hard side of it.

Klaus Karttunen

CONTENTS

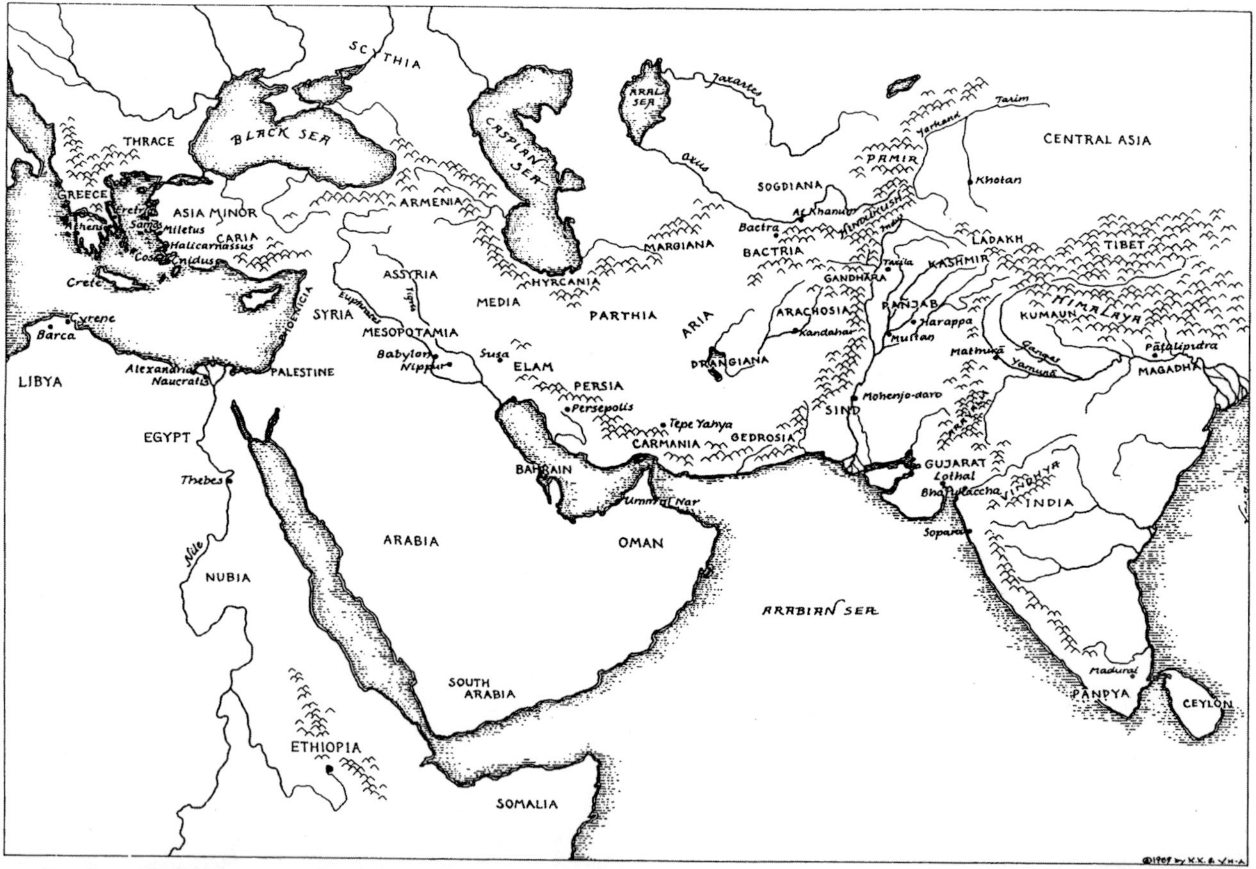
SCYTHIA
THRACE
BLACK SEA
CASPIAN SEA
ARAL SEA
Jaxartes
Oxus
Tarim
Yarkand
CENTRAL ASIA
PAMIR
Khotan
SOGDIANA
Ai Khanum
HINDUKUSH
Indus
GREECE
Eretria
Athens
Samos
ASIA MINOR
Miletus
CARIA
Halicarnassus
Cos
Cnidus
Crete
ARMENIA
Bactra
BACTRIA
MARGIANA
LADAKH
TIBET
KASHMIR
Taxila
GANDHARA
HYRCANIA
ASSYRIA
Tigris
Euphrates
MEDIA
PARTHIA
ARIA
ARACHOSIA
PANJAB
Harappa
KUMAUN
HIMALAYA
Cyrene
Barca
PHOENICIA
SYRIA
MESOPOTAMIA
Multan
Kandahar
Mathurā
Ganges
Yamunā
Pātaliputra
MAGADHA
Babylon
Nippur
Susa
ELAM
DRANGIANA
LIBYA
Alexandria
Naucratis
PALESTINE
PERSIA
Persepolis
Mohenjo-daro
SIND
Tepe Yahya
EGYPT
CARMANIA
GEDROSIA
GUJARAT
Lothal
Bharukaccha
VINDHYA
INDIA
Thebes
BAHRAIN
Umm an-Nar
Sopara
Nile
NUBIA
ARABIA
OMAN
ARABIAN SEA
Madurai
PANDYA
CEYLON
SOUTH ARABIA
ETHIOPIA
SOMALIA
©1969 by K.K. & Y.H.-A.

I. INTRODUCTION

One of the central concepts of this book is Hellenism. Here it is used in the restricted sense, to signify the period from Alexander the Great to the rise of Rome to supremacy. The conception itself is old and commonly, though often somewhat vaguely used. It does not have its origins in classical antiquity, but was, in this sense, an invention of the 19th century, when it was introduced in order to signify an opposite to the (Greek) classical period.[1] Politically, it is often defined as extending from the death of Alexander (323 B.C.) to that of Cleopatra (30 B.C.). Culturally, however, it is commonly used of the Greek element in the Roman empire, too, and occasionally its sphere has even been extended to Byzantium. In any case, it is very useful, but here its use demands some further considerations towards providing a definition.

For Droysen Hellenism meant a transitional period between classical Greece and Christianity. After him, we must note that the term has not always been used wholly consistently in the scholarly literature in different languages (such as English, French, German) and the ideas attached to it are not always the same. For a Wilamowitz, Kaerst and Tarn[2] Hellenism may have been an essentially Greek phenomenon, but this was achieved by more or less ignoring its other constituent elements. We prefer therefore to follow such scholars as Momigliano and O. Murray.[3]

According to the definition accepted in the present volume, Hellenism is the mixed culture of the post-Alexander era, in which Greek civilization and the Greek (as well as Macedonian) people participated, but not alone. For instance in Egypt, Syria and Mesopotamia, local people and local traditions were as much a part of it as were the Greeks. In some fields, especially in religion, this led to mixed phenomena, which sometimes became known everywhere in the Hellenistic world (such as for instance the cults of Isis and Sarapis).

With this definition, I see no reason not to use the word Hellenism even east of the Tigris, in Parthia, Bactria and Northwestern India, as far as the Greeks[4] were concerned.

---

1 The word itself is Greek and was used in antiquity, not in the present sense, but only in the very special sense to signify the difference between the Greek-speaking, Hellenized Jews (Ἑλληνισταί) and the Aramaic-speaking, traditional Jews (Ἑβραῖοι), who still used Hebrew in their synagogue service (Momigliano 1975b, 112f.). The introduction of the modern term is generally assigned to the German historian J. G. Droysen (*Geschichte des Hellenismus* 1–2. 1836–43). See Momigliano 1975b, 109f. & 113f.

2 For these three, see Momigliano 1975b, 125f. Tarn, as he rightly notes, "saw his Graeco-Macedonians as precocious Englishmen and Scotsmen settling on colonial land." For Tarn's own views, see e.g. Tarn & Griffith 1952, 1ff. The spirit of Tarn is also seen in Schneider 1967, 841ff.

3 See further e.g. Davies 1984, 263, Will in Will & Klein 1988, 387ff.

4 Here Greek also includes Macedonians, when not separately mentioned, as the original difference between the two peoples was rapidly disappearing everywhere in the Hellenistic world. For the

The fact that mutual interaction and influence with local people often took place to a great extent does not make the civilization un-Hellenistic,[5] no, rather the exact opposite. Accepting the Graeco-Bactrian and Indo-Greek kingdoms of Bactria and India as Hellenistic does not mean to deny or even belittle the Iranian and Indian elements in them, which were of course considerable.

* * *

Now we must consider our sources. The literary sources for the Graeco–Indian relations of the Hellenistic period fall naturally into two major categories – Western (Greek and Latin) and Indian. Only occasionally can they be supplemented by others. In this connection it is perhaps also in order to mention that, as I fancy that my readers will include both Indologists and classical scholars, I feel myself entitled sometimes to state even such facts which for an insider in one field may seem rather trivial. I shall begin with the classical sources.

The great majority of Hellenistic authors have for the most part been preserved only in fragments quoted in later literature. For our purpose the most important are the historians of Alexander and the Hellenistic ambassadors in India. Further material is found especially in geography and the natural sciences (chapters IV and V).

The number of historians writing on Alexander's life and career is exceptionally large. In addition to later sources, we know of more than twenty more or less contemporary accounts. There must also have been several of which we do not have any knowledge.[6] Quite a number of the known authorities had themselves participated in Alexander's campaigns. However, all their works are without exception lost and known only through fragments, and in a few cases only have we enough of them to form an idea of the author and of his work. I shall name only briefly these authors, as I have discussed them more fully on an earlier occasion.[7]

Let us begin with **Ptolemaeus**,[8] the *Soter*, the king and general, who wrote an exact and factual account of military events during the campaigns. Nearly everything that we know of his book comes from Arrianus. In the *FGrH* (number 138) we have no less than 35 fragments from him (including 5 *incerta*). Nine of them refer to India, but they only

---

dichotomy in Greek opinion concerning the status of Macedonians in the time of Philip and Alexander see e.g. Will in Will & Klein 1988, 385ff.

5 As suggested by Narain 1957, 10f. There are parallels in other directions, e.g. Meroe in the south.

6 Pearson 1960, 7. Without Arrianus, we would have a very poor idea of Ptolemaeus, and the still extant history of Curtius is never mentioned at all in other classical sources (Brunt 1984, 543).

7 Karttunen 1989a, 89ff. with references, especially to Pearson 1960. See also Bosworth 1988a.

8 See also e.g. Kornemann 1935, Pearson 1960, 188ff., and Pédech 1984, 215ff. In order to avoid confusion, I refer to the members of the Macedonian dynasty of Egypt as *Ptolemaeus* and to the scientist of the Roman Imperial period as Claudius *Ptolemy*. For other names I have generally preferred the original (for Greek Latinized) forms and use modern equivalents only in a few cases (e.g. Pliny, but Aristoteles).

rarely contain any information about the country. The old general – probably he was writing at an advanced age – concentrated solely on military operations, and without omitting his own, often important, part in them. Questions of ethnography and nature, so common in the works of his colleagues, are completely lacking. His fragments are thus important for the history of Alexander (although they occasionally may elapse into propaganda),[9] but hardly for India and Indo-Western relations.

Another companion of Alexander was the Greek **Aristobulus**.[10] Of his history (*FGrH* 139) we have 58 fragments, 15 of them on India. It is valuable especially because of his many observations on ethnography and nature, for which he was much used by Strabo, and will be often referred to in the following pages.

Ptolemaeus and Aristobulus were the main authorities used by Arrianus in his *Anabasis*, and therefore have been held responsible for the most reliable historical account, in opposition to the so-called Vulgate tradition (of Diodorus, Curtius, Plutarch and Justinus), probably going back to Cleitarchus. Both wrote at an advanced age (Aristobulus was one of the famous long-livers), and apparently in order to correct their predecessors.[11]

This was perhaps also the relation between **Nearchus**, the factual admiral,[12] and **Onesicritus**, the pupil of the Cynic philosopher Diogenes, whose work was often much criticized and despised, but also widely read.[13] While Onesicritus wrote a full history, or rather a kind of account of development, of Alexander, Nearchus seems to have restricted himself to the summit of his own career in Alexander's service, the riverine and coastal voyage of Alexander's fleet under his command. At the beginning, a description of India was also given. It was an important source for Strabo and Arrianus. The remains of Nearchus are given by Jacoby in *FGrH* 133 (with 29 fragments and five incerta, more than twenty dealing with India), those of Onesicritus in *FGrH* 134 (with 39 fragments, approx. 21 on India). Both were leading figures in the naval venture on the Arabian Sea, and in chapter II.4 we shall meet them again and some of their lesser-known companions.

Another eye-witness of the campaign was **Chares** of Mitylene (*FGrH* 125),[14] who held the office of chamberlain or officer in charge of Alexander's audiences. As far as his fragments (19, including some four on India) allow us to judge, he was neither particularly well informed nor much interested in facts of history or science. Instead, he wrote a collection of reminiscences and anecdotes showing an interest in such topics as the details of festivities, various items of food and drink, furniture and dress, and probably foreign customs. It seem illustrative that he is mainly known through Athenaeus and was never mentioned by Arrianus.

---

9 See Brunt 1983, 564ff.

10 On him see e.g. Pearson 1960, 150ff., and Pédech 1984, 331ff.

11 Pearson 1960, 152, and Brunt 1983, 554f.

12 Much has been written about Nearchus and his work. See e.g. Pearson 1960, 112ff., and Pédech 1984, 159ff., about his Indian fragments also Vofchuk 1982c.

13 For Onesicritus see e.g. Pearson 1960, 83ff., and Pédech 1984, 71ff., about his Indian fragments also Vofchuk 1986.

14 Pearson 1960, 50ff.

Cleitarchus (*FGrH* 137), the favourite of the reading public, had most probably not himself participated in Alexander's campaigns.[15] It has even been suggested that he wrote considerably later, but Badian has shown that he was probably a contemporary.[16] But even so, to quote Badian, "veracity is not his greatest attested virtue", in fact his history was mentioned as an example of the disreputed rhetorical style of historical writing. Nevertheless, his fragments (36 and some *incerta*, 10 or 11 on India) contain some interesting notes on India. It seems that they were partly derived from Onesicritus and Nearchus.[17]

India is also mentioned among the few fragments of such little-known authors as **Baeto** the Bematist (*FGrH* 119 with 5 certain fragments, 4 on India)[18] and **Polycleitus** of Larisa (*FGrH* 128 with 11 fragments, 2 on India). Both accompanied Alexander, and the latter seems to have written a long history, as one fragment (F 1) refers to his book VIII, but the few fragments do not allow us to form any good picture of him. Pliny mentions him together with Nearchus and Onesicritus, and some of his fragments deal with geography and nature.[19] From the rest of known Hellenistic historians of Alexander, nothing on things Indian is preserved.

It is something of a pity that we are so poorly informed on the (more or less) contemporary anti-Alexander literature. It was mostly written by Greeks, who still well remembered that Alexander and his father Philip had put an end to the freedom of Greece. The few fragments of **Ephippus** (*FGrH* 126) and **Nicobule** (*FGrH* 127) are thus extremely interesting, but at the same time do not reveal very much.[20] At a later period, Alexander was criticized mostly among certain philosophical schools.[21]

The rest of our other classical sources on India will be dealt with in later chapters: Megasthenes in chapter III, scientists (such as Aristoteles, Theophrastus, Eratosthenes, Hipparchus and Pliny) in chapter IV, later historians and other authors in VII.1. Instead, I must now discuss some general questions.

With these sources we must necessarily consider the peculiar philological problems encountered with fragmentary literature.[22] The fragments cannot make up for a lost original, of which we at best can only have an approximate idea. Very often we have

---

15 A somewhat unclear passage of Diodorus (2, 7) has sometimes been interpreted to this effect, but see Pearson 1960, 229ff. (and on Cleitarchus in general *ibid.*, 152ff. and 212ff.) and Badian 1965, 7ff.

16 Badian 1965, late 4th century also in Pédech 1984, 343. See Karttunen 1989a, 92f., with further references.

17 Pearson 1960, 225.

18 Cf. Aly 1957, 145ff., and Pearson 1960, 261. Of other Bematists, such as Diognetus (*FGrH* 120) we know still less. See also Baeto's uncertain F 6–7 and Jacoby's commentary on them in the *FGrH*.

19 Pliny, *N. H.* 1, 12, 13. On Polycleitus, see Pearson 1960, 70ff. In his few fragments, a picture arises of an author who promptly recorded curious and sensational details.

20 See Pearson 1960, 61ff. on Ephippus, and 67f. on Nicobule.

21 It seems that the Peripatetics, in remembrance of Callisthenes, were the most active critics, while the Stoics contributed much to the idealized conception of Alexander. Schachermeyr 1973, 609.

22 See also my discussion in Karttunen 1989a, 1989b, and 1991.

much less. Further, the value of fragments is not always the same. Some are exact quotations, some pretend to be such, but probably are not. Sometimes we only have a vague reference to the original source, and often it is difficult to say where the fragment ends, and whether it also contains some extraneous material. Generally ancient authors did not work in the same way as we do. Instead of having their desk full of books ready for checking references, they used to read the books first, and, when writing, rely on their memory for quotations. Occasionally they made notes, but often they seem to have relied most heavily on the author they happened to have read last.

But while we must always exercise our critical acumen with our attested fragments, we must also go beyond them. Sometimes we can reliably identify a fragment, though it is given without a reference. Keeping strictly to certainly attested fragments would often overly restrict our conception of an author. However, the scholarly literature of the 19th and 20th centuries is also full of examples where a fragment is confidently identified and ascribed to a particular author, although the case in fact might be very much open to criticism.[23] In the analysis, we must always consider two factors: the philological problems and peculiarities of the original work *and* of the work where the fragment is preserved. Often the matter is complicated by the fact that many fragments are quoted only indirectly, from some intermediate author, whose work is also lost to us. Often this intermediate source is not mentioned at all, and we can only surmise its existence.

Examples of both kind can be pointed out in the transmission of Onesicritus. Pliny quotes him quite openly through Juba, but only a comparison of corresponding passages of Strabo and Arrianus (*Indica*) shows that these two authors were probably quoting him (and others like Ctesias) through Eratosthenes.[24] However, a word of warning is again in place. Especially in late 19th-century philology it was often customary not to allow the slightest deviation or incongruency in a direct quotation. Therefore, a great number of intermediate sources were suggested in order to explain what were perhaps mere slips of memory on the part of the authors.

With all these words of warning the following table seems perhaps trivial. But allowing all differences between individual fragments it has the merit of indicating who might have actually read and used our Hellenistic authors and who only occasionally quote them, most probably through an intermediary. I have included Megasthenes, who will be fully discussed in chapter III.

23 See e.g. Pearson 1960, 187.

24 Brunt 1983, 445. This seems more likely than Pédech's claim (1984, 166) that Arrianus quoted Ctesias from Nearchus. It is questionable whether Nearchus knew Ctesias' work at all.

	Aristobulus	Nearchus[25]	Onesicritus	Cleitarchus	Megasthenes[26]
Fragments[27]	70	39	41	36	54
Fragments on India[28]	(16)	(28)	(27)	(14)	nearly all
Coming from:					
Aelianus	–	–	2 (2)	4 (4)	3
Arrianus	35 (4)	11 (10)	2 (2)	–	18
Athenaeus	5 (1)	–	–	4 (–)	1
Curtius	–	–	–	2 (2)	–
Pliny	–	4	9 (6)	5 (3)	7
Plutarch	11 (2)	–	6 (3)	2 (–)	1
Strabo	16 (9)	22 (15)	17 (12)	5 (3)	18

While the collections of fragments are very handy to use, they also contain some dangers. First, even with the best collections, we can never be certain that they contain all that is relevant. Even such a venerable work as Jacoby's *FGrH* can occasionally be added to. But there is also a more fatal source of error. Too often the fragments are taken as an equivalent of the work itself, too easily is their different transmission, their varying worth, exactness and reliability forgotten. One must always look at where a fragment was quoted, by whom it was quoted, and *why* it was quoted, to be conscious of all the philological problems and peculiarities of the authors who have preserved the fragments.

While the beginning of the Roman Empire forms the chronological limit for our study, though not always too strictly followed, later (Roman Imperial) authors are also important for us. In most cases only they represent the extant literature, and Hellenistic authors are preserved merely in fragments found in these later works. Also, they often refer to the earlier period so that we might be able to ascribe a certain piece of information to the Hellenistic period, although we might have no idea of the original source. The books on history (such as Diodorus, Curtius and Arrianus) and science (such as Strabo, Aelianus and Pliny) have preserved the major part of our knowledge of the historians of Alexander and of Megasthenes, though Diodorus and Curtius rarely name their sources. Scholars and antiquarians such as Pliny, Plutarch and Athenaeus are real treasure houses of fragments. Most of them will be discussed in later chapters, but some special cases demand our attention here. The other viewpoint, the position of these Imperial authors themselves as sources of information on India, in relation to their own time and audience, is purposely avoided here as it will be one of the themes in the next volume of our studies.

The history of **Diodorus**, like other works of the Roman period (e.g. Strabo, Pliny, and Arrianus) will thus be discussed on its own in the next volume. Even now, however,

25 The long F 1, excerpt in Arrianus' *Indica*, makes the comparison here rather distorted.

26 In addition comes the long F 4 from Diodorus, but one can never be quite sure whether all really goes back to Megasthenes.

27 Parallel fragments (type 1a & 1b in the *FGrH*) are here counted separately.

28 Including the Paropamisadae and the Gedrosian coast.

I must point out that though Diodorus most certainly was such a notorious compiler as he has been presented in scholarly literature and never better than his sources (in fact, few were, but Diodorus often succeeded in being much worse), the old tenet that he washim always dependent on a single source in each particular passage, is untenable in its most rigorous form. A comparison of his excursus on India (2, 35–42) with the fragments of Megasthenes clearly shows that the Hellenistic ambassador's work was much used, though never mentioned by name. But at the same time there are passages which are incompatible with Megasthenes, but easily derived from some other author, e.g. Onesicritus.[29] I wholly agree that he never collated sources as did Strabo and Arrianus, not even glued together excerpts as did Pliny and Aelianus, but even the worst compiler, who nevertheless had read several books, could hardly always refrain from adding something from memory. And at least at one point we can, with Murphy (1989, 55), congratulate Diodorus' common-sense (which he did not always show elsewhere in his work) that he left out of his account all fabulous peoples, though Megasthenes could have provided ample material in this respect, too.

Among the sources for the Hellenistic period an important, although rather complicated, authority is Flavius **Philostratus**. In the *Life of Apollonius of Tyana* he described at length the Indian travels of his hero, supposedly in 43/44 A.D.[30] At present we may leave aside the vexed question of the authenticity of the diary of Damis, the companion of Apollonius, to whom Philostratus refers as his main authority. On the one hand, a reading of the *Life* shows that it contains, in the form given to it by Philostratus, much that cannot come from a real travel journal.[31] Some passages might be simply concocted by the author, but from our viewpoint it is more important that our text also contains much that can be traced back to earlier literature on India. There is also much material which clearly belongs to the first century A.D., exactly to the period when Apollonius is supposed to have visited India, and neither to Philostratus' own time in the early third century A.D., nor to the fourth/third centuries B.C., the time of Alexander's historians and Megasthenes.[32] But in addition our text contains much that is derived from Megasthenes,[33] from Alexander's historians (who are sometimes even referred to by name), and even from

29 See e.g. the note on the text in the new translation by Murphy (1989). This question will be discussed more fully in my future volume on India and Rome.

30 On Apollonius' Indian travels, see Smith 1914 (331f. on the date) and Charpentier 1934 (with some additional notes by Johnson, 1935). Dani (1986, 69) suggests 46 A.D.

31 The pepper mountains between the Indus and the Ganges. Travel to the sea with the Ganges on the right and the Hyphasis on the left side. The Hyphasis pouring its waters directly into the sea through gorges and rapids. Not to speak of the marvels, which anyway are literary embellishment probably added by Philostratus, but often drawn from early Greek sources on India (such as Ctesias).

32 So e.g. the description of Taxila, dated with the help of the first-century earthquake (Marshall 1951, 63f.) and the fact that a prince with an apparently Parthian name, Phraotes, was ruling there (Smith 1914, 335). The Indian etymology (*apratihata*, actually met in a Kharoṣṭhī coin legend of Gondophares) suggested by Herzfeld (1932, 112f.) and, after him, Tarn (1951, 341) seems to me unconvincing. Wholly speculative is Breloer (1939, 290ff.), who sees in Phraotes a veiled account of Candragupta going back to Megasthenes.

33 Breloer 1939, however, goes much too far.

Ctesias and Scylax.[34] The problem is that the sources are rarely named, and it is not always an easy task to find them out.

Another complicated case is the legendary literature on Alexander. Especially *Alexander's Letter to Aristoteles* clearly contains much Hellenistic material on India,[35] but in the present study it is only used rarely. Although Gunderson (1980) has made a good beginning with the *Letter*, it still needs a special study, which cannot be attempted here. The text of Pseudo-Callisthenes in its various recensions occasionally contains material going back to the Hellenistic age, but it is often hopelessly intertwined with later material. The interesting booklet of Pseudo-Palladius, incorporated in the *Alexander Romance*, belongs wholly beyond our period, and will be taken up only at a later phase of our studies.

For readers uninitiated into the peculiarities of classical literature I should like to point out some further facts, important for our understanding of them and thus for the present study. They are more or less connected with the age-old question of reliability.

Some ancient critics have liberally used the verdict on a writer generally translated by the word "liar". 'To lie' is one of the meanings of Greek ψεύδειν, indeed, but in the context of ancient literary and scholarly criticism a more exact rendering would be 'to write fiction'. And the boundary between fiction and non-fiction did not always run on the same lines as with us, and it was also not at all as distinct as with us. There was, for instance, a well-established, though also, and from our viewpoint rightly, criticized, school of writing history, "in which it was recognized that the author could tell lies for the sake of effect".[36] Among historians of Alexander it was represented by Callisthenes' and Cleitarchus' highly dramatized accounts. The criticism came only occasionally, from more sober authors. For a long time Cleitarchus was the most popular among the historians of Alexander. Ptolemaeus and Aristobulus in their factual accounts probably lacked elegance and the ability to win over their audience, at least they are only rarely referred to before Arrianus, who chose them as his major sources.[37]

Even when the main purpose of writing history was not in dramatic effect and entertainment, but in a more or less factual account of what had happened, it was a part of literary routine to use certain stylistic means. The most important was the use of speeches in order to explain plans and motives. The purpose of these speeches was only to explain these and the idea of the author on them, and it was of no importance whether he actually knew what, for instance, Alexander had really said on a given occasion. What he wrote was his (or his source's) opinion of what could or should have been said on that occa-

34 Wonder stories in *V. Ap.* 3, 1ff. and 3, 45ff., see Karttunen 1989a, 67f., and Reese 1914, 90ff.

35 And even earlier, e.g. from Ctesias, see Karttunen 1989a, 95 (note) and Gunderson 1980. Gunderson dates the letter itself to the Hellenistic period. Personally, I like to stay on the safe side and accept no early dates without clear evidence. Of course, the possibility is there. See also Merkelbach 1954.

36 Pearson 1960, 19.

37 Pearson 1960, 20f. Among other early, and important, representatives of the dramatizing school were Duris of Samos and Phylarchus, whom we shall meet again in chapter VI.1. An account of classical ideas on historical style is given by Lucianus (*Quomodo historia conscribenda sit*).

sion. He wrote the speech in order to convey to his audience as good an idea as possible of the situation.[38]

Another important fact is that the rules of reference were not the same as with us. A reference was generally given only when one was criticizing one's predecessors. When the author agreed, he could silently use them, and nobody was offended. Often it also seems that named criticism was meant to conceal the actual dependence of the critic on the work criticized. The concept of plagiarism, however, was only invented in a late period, and because of this earlier usage, it was very much used by the late critics of classical antiquity. An additional feature, already mentioned above, was that even when cited, the source was not necessarily, and needed not be, directly used, and an intermediary was only mentioned when there was a need to comment on his opinions.[39]

The scholarly literature dealing with Greek and Latin historical, ethnographic and geographical accounts of foreign countries can be roughly divided into two categories. Some deal all the time with the classical world and its literary traditions and styles, while others refer to literary, epigraphic and archaeological sources of the country discussed. In the first case, everything can be seen as hardly more than exotic fiction, in the second, an ancient text often tends to come suspiciously near a modern report or study. This difference of interpretation depends on different viewpoints. When the ethnographic writings of antiquity are studied as a part of classical literature or science, read and cited by an educated audience, it is easy and important to stress their role as literary works in a classical context. It is easy to show their dependence on literary predecessors, the frequency of topoi and *interpretatio Graeca*, the importance of the theoretical framework, and the rarity of real objectivity and independent attempts at obtaining fresh knowledge. On the other hand, this kind of literary approach seems hardly adequate for a scholar who digs in the classical sources in order to cull at least some valuable scraps and hints of information about peoples and cultures otherwise very poorly known. A scholar interested in ancient Ethiopia, Arabia, India, Iran, Central Asia, Russia, or Germany can hardly be content solely with literary predecessors, topoi, *interpretatio Graeca*, and theory, when he is able to verify some part of the account from independent local evidence. But then he is also often too eager to accept as straightforward evidence something which can be truly understood only in connection with its literary context.

Both these viewpoints are inevitable. Both are important and useful, and can provide valuable results. Both are also defective, when used alone. Therefore, we should attempt to pay attention to both. Alone, the first tends to isolate the classical world wholly from its surroundings, but the conclusions drawn by the second without acknowledging the first can often be highly suspect.

---

[38] See Brunt 1983, 528ff. on speeches in Arrianus. A good occasion for such speeches was, for instance, the dramatic turning back at the Hyphasis (see Arrianus, *Anab.* 5, 25–27, and Curtius 9, 2–3).

[39] An interesting parallel, in a case where both original sources and the intermediaries are preserved to us in their entirety, as printed books, can be found in the dissertations of the 17th century. At least in Academia Aboensia (University of Turku) it was a common habit to give references only to the original sources (e.g. a classical author), though the sum of them clearly shows that they were just culled from a then modern handbook, where all these references were given together.

* * *

The second major source of the present study is the Indian literary evidence. While detailed problems of interpretation will again be occasionally discussed in the following chapters, a general survey of these sources and the possibilities of using them as material for our period is given here. This is often a very complicated question indeed. It is well known that the literary chronology of ancient India is very vague, and often we cannot define the origin of a literary work even with the accuracy of a century. Nevertheless, in the historical context we should attempt to use contemporary sources and when not, always take into account the chronological problems involved with later (in India often much later) evidence.

An important dividing line is here the rise of the great Gupta dynasty in the 4th century A.D. The Indo-Greek, Saka, Indo-Parthian and Kushan rule in the Northwest, the flourishing trade of West and South India with the Roman West, the considerable development of Indian art, literature, science and religion during the centuries immediately preceding the Guptas make Gupta India an entirely different country from that of the Mauryas. Therefore, what is pre-Gupta is important to us, and what is not must be handled with great care.

The most ancient literary monument of India is the great religious corpus of the **Veda**.[40] The major part of it is certainly much older than our period, the bulk of it (most of the Saṃhitā and Brāhmaṇa texts) seems to belong to the first part of the first millennium B.C. Therefore they do not concern us much here. But the Vedic period did not end abruptly; the last part of it, that of the Sūtra literature, went on even to the first millennium A.D. While the oldest Dharmasūtras (such as Gautama and Baudhāyana, perhaps also Vasiṣṭha) probably go back to the period before Alexander, some later ones (such as Āpastamba and Viṣṇu) often belong precisely to our period. But here we meet also the general difficulty of ancient Indian literary history. There are no exact dates at all, and a relative chronology, in addition to being often open to criticism, generally allows a fluctuation of several centuries. On the other hand, the manner of transmission, as oral material, with great weight put on preserving the exact wording, makes the Vedic literature an exceptionally good source for early India, while many other genres have been open to interpolation until a much later period.

The **great epics** of India, the *Mahābhārata* and the *Rāmāyaṇa*, belong in their present form to a later period. The critical study of their text cannot easily or with any degree of reliability go beyond the recensions of the Gupta period, and even the attempt to reconstruct these archetypal recensions from the wide sea of manuscripts, dividing into many different, often geographical sub-recensions, by producing critical editions has not succeeded without attracting serious criticism. Nevertheless, the critical editions of both epics, published in Poona and Baroda, offer the best available texts for historically orien-

---

40 See also Karttunen 1989a, 153ff.